An Expat's Guide to Thailand

Thailand Expat Immigration, Housing and Living Options,
Work & Business, Family & Education, Retirement,
Relocation Tips, Taxes & Banking, Essential Expat Guide
and Much More!

By Tess Downey

Foreword

Whenever faced with moving to a new country to relocate, whether it is for purposes of wanting a change of scene, or because of the necessities of work, one will have to do the needful and research up-to-date and trustworthy information on the different features and aspects of living a life in a different country as an expat. There are many important questions to be asked in relation on how to go about the procedures of securing the necessary paperwork, the neighborhoods you would need to check out for your lodging, schools to look up for the kids, security level of the city, and other important little bits of information that will allow you a smooth transfer and transition.

Gathering information from different sources can be painstaking and time-consuming but these are necessary things which need to be carried out, unless you are the adventurous sort who would sell the Jeep, sublet the apartment and quit their job to head into the great unknown. Moving from one neighborhood can already be a daunting task with stuff sort, box and label. Moving to another country will take double the planning. This is especially so if you are a family up and relocating to another part of the world. Thailand is no different in this case. In fact there are quite a number of things that need to be considered when thinking about moving to this beautiful country in Asia.

Table of Contents

Introduction to Thailand

Knowing the various things about living in Thailand as an expat is what the information we have compiled here for you to aid you along your journey to a new life in alluring Thailand. This Thailand expat guide is meant to give the individual wishing to move to the Land of Silk, the most recent information about relocating there available.

Find out about the requirements you will need for the new chapter of your life by squaring away the most important details of your move. Finding more about some of the communities and neighborhoods you could potentially be joining, is one of the most important bits to sort out for any person wanting to relocate to another country. Sure, time and experience being in the country will eventually get you into the rhythm of the pulse, but everyone needs a leg up because it just makes life a little easier.

Apart from places to stay other things you will need to know are basic laws and stipulations on foreign nationals wishing to make Thailand their home. We have compiled some of the most immediate details and bits that would help you out in making life a wee bit easier. Thailand is rich in culture and tradition. They are generally warm, hospital people open to the possibilities and offerings of today's modern times without forgetting their rich history as they move to the step of the world around them.

Life in Thailand can be promising, enriching and fulfilling if you know what is expected of you as a permitted long-term visitor. It would also be in your gain to get ahead by learning all that you can about this beautiful kingdom you have chosen to call your new home and where you can build a life you have worked toward.

Chapter One: General Facts about Thailand

Thailand prides itself for being an autonomous country which was never successfully colonized by stronger, well-muscled countries, despite the few territorial losses to a couple of Western countries in the 15th century. Thailand is the only Southeast Asian country that has enjoyed freedom from colonization by any European nation. It continues to entice people from all over the world to visit her shores for a myriad of reasons.

People from far and wide head to the majestic country, once lauded as country of multiple kingdoms, for business, work, studies, marriage, to visit or to relocate. Rightfully so, because it does have the perks of the fast moving modern-day luxuries of technology mixed into the deep cultural love and heritage of the people for their country.

The eclectic mix of the country is apparent in the landscape of the big cities of Thailand. Spotted smattered all over these big city landscapes, as one passes through any one of the massive, concrete autobahns and sky-highways, travellers would note the apparent importance of the love for country and its deep and long association with Buddhism. Peppered throughout the city landscapes are Thai flags flying high and flying proud that anyone new to the country would think there was some sort of festivity they had stumbled upon. This show of country-love becomes more apparent as your stay progresses. Beautiful temples and elaborate shrines erected in reverence are plentiful in Thailand, with an estimated 40,000 temples all over the country.

They are some of the most welcoming of people and are happy to help in ways they would be able to (given the generally very little English spoken). Thailand is classified as a newly developed economy because of its reliance on exports such as electronics, machinery, car parts and food goods. Making up the leading contributors of earnings and economy are the manufacturing, agricultural and tourism sectors. The scents and smells of the food, which to the rest of the world is rare, almost permeate the air of heavily populated areas.

Thailand History

A common belief on the origins of the Thai people is that they originated in the southeastern region of China in 650 Ad. This was when the Kingdom of Nanchao was established. Stories talk about the migration of these people to the south in the 13th century to an area now known to be a northern region of Thailand. Here in this region the capital called Sukhothai was established. During the Sukhothai period, the first kingdom in Thailand, the Thais developed their own language and perfected their architecture. This was also the time of a burst of Thai art and culture became more apparent and alive. The invention of Thai script soon followed marking a milestone in the history of the country and people. This was when the first written record of Thai history came about. The Kingdom thrived and flourished for the next century but eventually succumbed to ruins when the more powerful kingdom, from the area upstream of the Chao Phraya River, Ayutthaya arose in the mid-14th century.

The period of the Ayutthaya kingdom became a period of prominence, affluence, and great influence. It was backed up with a military force. It was the kingdom which set off trading with countries of the West. It was also during the period of Ayutthaya when the Thais and Burmese vied for territory. The kingdom of Ayutthaya enjoyed over four centuries of glory until its capital was lost to the Burmese during an invasion in 1767 AD.

The control of the Burmese did not last very long since the major military figures were able to flee south toward the Chao Phraya River.

One of those who were able to tromp to the safe zone of the Chao Phraya River was General Tak Sin. Him, along with his followers, set up residence in a city by the Chao Phraya River called ThonBuri. Once they were able to plan out their move, General Tak Sin and his men drove the Burmese away from Ayutthaya. By this time the city of Ayutthaya had already been ravaged to such a horrible extent. Seeing the futility of rebuilding, General TakSin made the decision to move the capital of Ayutthaya to ThonBuri. Upon the relocation of the capital, the General then went on to declare himself King TakSin of the Taksin Dynasty. The TakSin dynasty was a short one and there were no other king after his death in 1782 AD.

After the death of King TakSin, General Chakri transferred the capital of the country to a location across the Chao Phraya River, to Bangkok and proclaimed himself King Rama I of the Chakri Dynasty. This would be the reign that would start the Rattanakosin period. This dynasty is what continues on to this present day. His Majesty King Bhumibol (Rama IX) has reigned over the kingdom of Thailand since 1946. He is known not only for being the longest serving monarch in Thai history; he is also the longest reigning monarch in the world.

The country had always been known as Siam until the end of the reign of King Rama IX. Siam was changed to Thailand in 1939, which reflect of the nation's pride on being the only country in the region of Southeast Asia that dodged the bullet on being colonized.

Let's move into the present and your business at hand. As you read on you will find helpful information in relation to what you need to know about your new home, for now.

Chapter Two: Upon Arrival in Thailand

Suvarnabhumi is Bangkok's International Airport located km east of Bangkok, in the Bang Phli district of the Samut Prakan Province. The trip downtown, through the wide and winding expressways, takes less than an hour. This fairly new airport opened in September 2006 and is currently Bangkok's main international airport. The name Suvarnabhumi means The Golden Land and was ordained by His Majesty, The King.

The passenger terminal is a sole building which serves both domestic and international flights and passengers. There are over 80 international airlines serviced by the Suvarnabhumi Airport from all over the world and also accommodate a few domestic airlines.

Don Muaeng is the second airport in Bangkok and used to be Bangkok's International Airport for more than 80 years. Domestic carriers were encouraged to move back to Don Muaeng International Airport because of the congestion at Suvarnabhumi. At present, Don Muaeng serves the main hub for low-cost domestic airlines like Nok Air and Thai Air Asia. Flights from Hong Kong, Singapore, Jakarta and other international countries are also served by the Don Muaeng domestic airport.

Before Leaving the Airport

Aside from making sure that you have all your personal effects, luggage and belongings, take stock of all your travel documents and identification papers, especially if travelling as a group of people, i.e. your family. Once you have sure that you have all of these in check make certain that you have enough Thai baht before exiting the airport doors. This is something you want to do at any of the many foreign exchange booths scattered around the airport.

The airport is a convenient place to not only get your money exchanged to Thai baht and where you can get a fair rate exchange. You would also be able to get hooked back up and get online with the 3G services offered by different Thai telecoms. The airport is also a place where you could possibly get some of your more favored trappings like snacks, cigarettes, perfume and merchandise from home or other parts of the world.

Duty Free and Eats

As you exit the hatch from the airplane, you will be greeted by miles of merchandise from all over the world. You may want to grab a quick chance to grab up some of your favorite snacks, perfume, cosmetics, and toiletries that may not be readily available in the city. There are also a number of restaurants where you can duck into after a long flight where you can dig into a simple meal or get the first taste of Thailand.

Free Airport Wi-Fi, Public Phones and Thai SIM Cards

You can request for an hours 'worth of free Wi-Fi at the Suvarnabhumi International Airport. Place your request and get help setting your phone up at airport information counters. Conveniently located in both the passenger terminal and the concourse buildings are public telephones available for you to make domestic calls. Local toll call rates are 1 baht for a 3-minute call to landlines. Mobile call rates are 3 baht per minute. Mobile Phone Service counters are conveniently located outside the arrival gate on the 2nd floor of the passenger terminal. Airport reception can help you set up your mobile phones and configure your phone settings. Available services from mobile operators such as AIS, DTAC and TrueMove are choices you have. You can conveniently buy SIM cards and register for your choice of mobile services at these airport counters.

Foreign Exchange

Assuming that you have made previous arrangements with your bank to be able to withdraw funds from your overseas account from Thailand, you will also want to make sure that you have enough funds to finance the first few weeks of your stay is more than needful. You will be able to find foreign exchange counters located inside the airport, making it convenient and safe for you to change currencies. You don't want to be sitting in a cab speeding toward an unfamiliar, albeit exciting, city and not have the cash to pay for your fare.

Transportation into the City

There are a number of methods for you to get into the city that you can choose to use. A person who has been lucky enough to have visited the country often enough may have been able to find alternate and less costly methods of finding their way into the hub of Bangkok. The novice of course will not be as savvy and could most probably run into some problems, starting with a language barrier. Therefore if you had not made any arrangements with your travel agent for transportation services, your last chance to do that is at the Suvarnabhumi, where there are transport service counters who can accommodate your travel needs into the city as well as any arrangements you would need to

make for a car.

Chapter Three: Generalities - All Bits Important

Each country and the people of the land, have unique qualities and distinct differences from one another. You will be joining a country that has had a long history of tradition and culture that is now a bit more simplified with the union of the country. Take a bit of time getting to know the country who will be graciously hosting your stay in this magnificent kingdom of Thailand.

Population and People

Based on the estimations of the United Nations, the population of Thailand, to date, is 69,141,959. Thailand makes up 0.91% of the world's population, and has a population density of 135 per Km2 or 351 people per mi2. It has total land area is 510,890 Km2 or 197,256 sq. miles. The urban population of the country is at 52.6%, with a headcount of 36,419,724 people in 2018. The number of migrants in Thailand has remained at a steady 19, 444 from 2016 to this year (2018).

Thais make up approximately 75 % of the country's population. 14% of the populace is made up of ethnic Chinese, with the rest of the population comprised by other ethnic groups which include 4% of Malay Muslims, 4% of Pakistanis and Indians, 1.3% Khmer, 1.3% Kui or Soai, 1.3% Karen. Eight percent of the country's population is made up of the northern hill tribes. There are also about 20 million Lao Isan living in the Northeastern region of Thailand which are thought to be different from other Thai ethnic groups but are nonetheless Thais.

And because of differences in the environment and geographical features of the country, residents in each region of the country tend to have their own characteristics and distinct appearances,

Religion

The landscape of Thailand, once you arrive, is rife and rich with the many temple complexes scattered throughout the city and the countryside. It is the most heavily populated Buddhist country in the world with an estimated 93.6 % of Thais being Theravada Buddhists. Wats, or Buddhist temples as the Thais call them, as well as monks in flowing saffron robes can be spotted almost anywhere. The Malays, that mostly lives in the southern part of Thailand with a small population found in the north of the country, makes up for the 4% of the Islamic followers. There are animist hill tribesmen, who follow the belief of all things having a soul, have recently converted to Christianity and who make up 0.9 percent of the country's population.

The rest of the population in Thailand are made up of Hindus (0.1%), Sikhs, Baha'i Faith amongst others that make up 0.6 percent of the belief systems in the country.

Even though the vast majority of the people of the country practice the official religion of the country, Theravada Buddhism, religious tolerance is customarily observed and protected in the country by the constitution of Thailand.

Time and Climate

There are no time zones in Thailand. Time in the country is 7 hours ahead of the Greenwich Mean Time and the country does not have daylight saving time.

Sunny beaches, lazy rivers, tropical fruit trees and the warmth of the sun on your skin are images that the mind conjures when thinking of Thailand. It is a country which enjoys warm days all year-round. It is a humid country in the tropics with the average temperature is approximately 29°C or 84°F and humidity is roughly 73 – 82%. However, the people of Thailand would say that there are three distinct seasons of the year; summer comes around in March and sticks around until about May; the rainy season is prevalent from around June to October; cooler weather is enjoyed around November to February. Any other time in between is warm and sunshine. It is no wonder that beaches in this country are continuously visited year in and out.

Language

There was a time when some Thai government's applied pressure on the various ethnicities of Thai people to turn their backs on customs traditionally revered and observed by the region they are native to, as well as the dialects spoken within the various tribes and regions for the more modern-day Thai culture that had been adapted. Law states that the Central Thai dialect was to be taught in all schools under government authority. Those who also wanted to hold a government position.

In the past, some Thai governments put great pressure on the various Thai peoples to forsake regional customs and tribal dialects. It was pressed upon the people that they should take up the more modern evolution of the Central Thai culture. The law states that the Central Thai dialect should be taught in all schools under the government administration. This went the same for any individual who looked to get a government seat, from the headsman of a village to the highest possible office to be held, all individuals who sought to have a position in government were to have mastery of the Central Thai dialect.

Despite these efforts to unify all tribes under one central umbrella of language and culture, the local dialects of regional areas remained to be spoken in markets, regional government offices, and schools. Central Thai or Siamese is the official national language of Thailand. The tonal language has a complex grammar, which makes it one of the more difficult languages to learn. To confound even more is, the written and spoken language can vary from each other occasionally. Given enough time, patience, diligence and practice, foreigners are able to learn the language and train their ear to get used to speaking and hearing it.

Electricity and Water

The electric current in Thailand is 220 volts, 50 Hz, using continental (two prong) style power points. Make it a point to avoid drinking or using tap water for food, this is especially if you have a sensitive stomach. Get a filter and fit your tap with one or purchase bottled water instead.

Business Hours

Knowing when to head out for chores, groceries and errands is something good for a new expat in the country to know. You will certainly get the hang of when what is open after a couple of months in the country. The Internet is still a good place to look up updates or schedule changes, but the ones most important to remember are pretty staple places that you will need to be aware of. Government offices are open 8.30 am – 4.30 pm Monday through Friday. Post offices are open between 8.30 am – 5.00 pm Monday through Friday.

Most banks are open from 8.30 am – 3.30 pm Monday through Friday and those located in the malls are open between 10.00 am – 8.00 pm every day. Big department stores are conveniently open from 10.00 am – 10.00 pm each day.

Currency

The standard monetary unit used in Thailand is the Thai Baht.

- 1 Baht is divided into a smaller unit called Satang
- 1 Baht = 100 Satangs

Thai baht banknotes are available in six denominations - 20, 50, 100, 500, and 1,000. Thai coins come in tokens of 25 and 50 Satangs, and 1, 2, 5, and 10 Baht. These coin tokens come in different sizes and forms, so it is actually wise to get used to them, because every Satang saved is a Satang earned. Avoid the hassle of shady businesses and take your business of exchanging foreign currency at your local or any commercial bank, currency exchange services, or authorized money changers.

Weight and Measurement

The standard measurement system in Thailand is the metric system (as the Thai to metric system)

- o   2 kueb (hand stretch) = 1sogg (elbow length)
- o   4 sogg = 1 wa (arm stretch)
- o   16 square sogg = 1 square wa
- o   100 square wa = 1 ngan
- o   400 square wa = 1 rai
- o   1 rai = 1,600 square metres
- o   100 square wa = 400 square metres

Chapter Four: Thailand Laws

Other than keeping your nose clean, there are still laws, and rules that a potential expat who intends to live and work in Thailand would need to know. The old adage of "ignorance of the law excuses no one" holds true for every individual so, as much as you will discover more about the laws of Thailand, we have highlighted some of the more immediate ones of which you will need to be absolutely aware.

Section 206 of the Penal Code states that Whoever commits any act of malice or insult to an object or a place of religious reverence of any community that would bring insult to the religion will be meted with a minimum of 1 year to a maximum of 7 years imprisonment or a fine of 2,000 to 14,000 baht or both.

Section 208.of the Thai penal code states that whoever dresses up or uses a symbol indicating that he is a Buddhist monk or novice, ascetic, OR anyone who dons garments or unlawfully pretends to be a clergyman of any religion so as to lead another person believe that he is such a person will be punished with incarceration not exceeding one year or a fine not exceeding 2,000 baht or both.

Tourists are able to get *Value Added Tax (VAT) Refunds.* To be eligible for a VAT Refund, the individual has to meet all of the following requirements:

- that you exit Thailand through an international airport

- that you are a non-Thai resident who has been in the country for no longer than 180 days and

- that you are not a pilot or cabin crew of any departing airline.

In addition to these, you will have to present your passport, along with a VAT Refund Application Form The VAT Refund Application form can be obtained online or at the airport. You will also need to present the original receipt(s) of goods you bought in Thailand, as well as the actual goods that were purchased.

Although widely notorious for being a tourism destination for sex, the country of Thailand passed an anti-prostitution law back in April of 1996. As of this writing, customers, procurers, owners of brothels, and any individual found to force or coerce children into prostitution, shall face tough and lengthy prison sentences along with paying massive fines for any sort of involvement in any kind of prostitution.

The ban on the sale of alcohol is observed in the country between 2pm and 5pm and again between midnight and 11am, every day of the week. So time your alcohol purchases. This alcohol ban regulation largely affects supermarkets and convenience chain stores, like 7-11 or Tops. This law is not always enforced at smaller, family-run shops and is pretty much common knowledge amongst locals.

Bans on alcohol and alcohol sale are strictly enforced by The Election Commission of Thailand on Election Days for the offices of Prime Minister and Senator, and includes advanced voting days. Over and above these stated times and special days of election period, the Government of Thailand has also been known to prohibit the sale of alcohol during religious holidays.

Tourists and new residents of Bangkok should be aware of the rules and regulations they are to adhere to in order to avoid being penalized and/or fined. Jaywalking and littering are offences to avoid in Thailand.

Street signs in Thai and English are posted almost everywhere. Consider these laws, as the Tourist Police will accost and slap charges on anyone breaking these laws.

Chapter Five: Visa Talk

It is a given that when traveling internationally we all need a passport. Passport is an internationally accepted verification of your identification at border passing and immigration throughout the world. It gives details of where you're from, your name, the validity of your passport, the port of your departure, and your visa. Visas work differently than passports because this shows the information of why you are traveling to any particular country. A visa also shows the length of time you plan to stay in that country.

There are a myriad of Thai visas available, and knowing which visa to apply for and figuring out which one suits your needs can be quite daunting and confusing. It is definitely not a straightforward process. There are a lot of stipulations in the small print and if you aren't guided well, or if you are not sure which one you'll need, you could face deportation.

Visas are typically given to individuals who seek to study or work abroad for a certain period of time. However those are not the only types of visas. Other visas available are many and range from business, temporary, work, study, marriage and retirement visas. This is a good time to find out about the different types of visas to avoid the possibility of being sent back to your home country and of course having to explain your unfortunate situation once you are deported back. Let's delve in a bit more and get a deeper understanding of the five most common types of Thai visas available for foreigners.

The Tourist Visa

Thailand has consistently been a tourist destination for many travelers because of the magnificent landscapes and historical sites. These make for some of the best photographs for your vacation albums. If this is the case, then read on to find out what you need to get ready to start the process.

For one to apply for a Thai tourist visa, you will need to have a passport with at least six months of validity remaining. You would also have to provide two passport-sized photos. At this point you would have already purchased your flights. Provision of a copy of your round trip tickets or confirmed itinerary is required.

Traveling individuals should also have proof that they have the proper amount funds that would cover their travel costs whilst in the country. You will have to show proof that you are able to fund your stay, a reasonable 20,000 Baht per person and 40,000 Baht per family.

There are two sorts of Thai tourist visas. A single entry visa allows you a stay of 3 months/60 days straight in the country. A six-month, multiple entry visa is a newer and by far, the better option. This 6-month visa gives you the convenience, permitting one to stay in Thailand for 60 days at a time, however, with multiple entries.

Application Requirements

In order to apply, you will need to have a passport with at least six months of remaining validity. You must also have two 4x6 passport photos. You must have already purchased the flights, providing a copy of your round trip tickets or your confirmed travel itinerary.

Application Process

A Thai tourist visa is one of the easiest visas to get because there are not too many requirements for the short visa permission. Locate the Thai embassy or consulate in your home country and put in an application there.

Thailand is a country of great and awesome adventures and it wouldn't be a surprise if you choose to stay longer. Once in Thailand, the traveler has an option to extend the visa twice. Each extension allows you an additional stay of 39 days and costs 1,900 baht for each request. The approval of the extension of stay request depends on the discretion of the immigration officer.

Visa Benefits

The advantages of the single entry visa is usually sufficient for those who have a travel-plan around the country that would take them longer than the more frequent 2-week visit.. This visa allows the traveler the luxury of seeing and spending 6-months in the country at a time, each stay necessitates leaving every 60 days. The perk of entering the country with this visa the allowed provisional stay of 60 days instead of the standard 30 on arrival. It allows you more time to enjoy more of the culture and sites of the country whilst waiting for upcoming festivals without having to go on the necessary visa run to buy time.

The Work or Business Visa (Non-Immigrant "B" Visa)

There are many individuals who go to Thailand for the purpose of obtaining jobs. These are usually people who teach English as a second language. Then there are those who get relocated to the country because of their jobs. Others go there to invest and then there are those who set up and run international business.

The B visa process is relatively easy to apply for, provided that you have the proper documents to present at the Royal Thai Embassies or Royal Thai Consulates-General in your country. An individual who is a holder of this sort of working visa and would like to work in Thailand would have to be given a work permit before they begin work. The visa fee for this type of visa is 2,000 Baht and is valid for a single-entry with three-month validity and 5,000 Baht for multiple entries with a one-year validity.

Keep in mind that this visa does not double as your work permit. The work permit must be obtained by the interested individual separately whilst in Thailand. This is usually carried out by the potential employer. Should you wish to work in Thailand, apply initially for the 90--day Non-Immigrant B Visa (under the employment category), from your country of residence. Your work permit application can then, ideally, be worked on during the initial 90-days of the validity of your visa. When the valid work permit has been obtained, you can then apply for the 1-year Non-Immigrant B visa in Thailand.

Once you have your work permit, you will have to report to any Thai Immigration Office every 90 days. Should you have to travel outside of the country, you will also need to obtain a re-entry permit. The convenience of this visa is that this visa can be renewed in the country.

Application Process

Those wishing to make Thailand a temporary home and be employed at the same time would have to present their Passport or travel document clearly stating a validity of not less than 6 months. A completed visa application form should be submitted along with a recent passport-sized photograph,of the applicant with dimensions of 4 x 6 cm, and taken within the past 6 months. The applicant is to provide evidence of adequate finances that would fund their stay in Thailand with a minimum of 20,000 Baht per person and 40,000 Baht per family. The work visa applicant is also to furnish the Thai embassy or consulate with a letter of approval from the Ministry of Labour. In order to get a letter of approval, the applicant's prospective employer in Thailand has to submit a Form WP3 at the Office of Foreign Workers Administration, Department of Employment, Ministry of Labour, or at the local Provincial Employment Office of their respective province.

For those who have had experience working in the country and are returning for another leg of work, they would have to provide a Copy of Work Permit issued by the Ministry of Labour along with an alien income tax or Por Ngor Dor 91. A foreign national who is granted a Non-Immigrant visa will be able to work in Thailand once they have been granted a work permit. Any foreign nationals found in violation of the Immigration Act B.E. 2522 (1979) relevant to taking up employment without work permit or the Royal Decree B.E. 2522 (1979) concerning holding employment in specifically restricted jobs and professions will be prosecuted and imprisoned or they could be fined, or face both consequences. The applicant has to apply for the work visa at the Thai Embassy/ Consulate in the country where they reside.

Alternatively, they can also apply in any country where there is a Thai Embassy or Consulate, other than Thailand. Initially a single-entry and multiple-entry visas are valid for three months. Multiple-entry visas are valid for 1 year, with stipulation to exit every 90 days. Make sure that your passport is valid for six months or more for a single entry. Passport with multiple entry visa must be valid for 18 months or more.

Visa Benefits

An individual who has been granted a multiple-entry B visa is allowed to stay in Thailand for 90 days. They will also have the luxury and convenience of opening a bank account and get a work permit. The B visa covers work relating to doing business in the country, to work in the country, to attend conferences, to conduct scuba diving courses, Muay Thai or kickboxing courses, massage courses and to teach English and other languages. This visa is suitable for individuals prospecting for business in the country. It is also suitable for those attending conferences and meeting with Thai companies. It is also suitable for those attending trade shows or seminars.

Retirement Visa

Thailand's yearlong tropical weather makes it a perfect haven for those who are looking to kick up their tired heels and enjoy a truly fruitful and more relaxing retirement. Whether you are looking to slow down or be on the go, the shores of Thailand is definitely one country to check out if you are looking to retire somewhere where life can afford you to sleep in a little later and call it a day, sooner. The retirement visa is not as laborious or painstaking as other more complicated visas and the government has even made online provisions for reporting.

Application Requirements

This visa is also known as the long stay visa, but is officially called the retirement visa or the non-immigrant "O-A" visa. In order to be eligible to apply for one, the individual must be at least 50 years old. The individual should also have a spotless criminal background, meaning, no record or criminal activity.

The individual should have a security deposit of 800,000 baht in a Thai bank account, or a monthly pension stipend of 65,000 baht, two months before the application for the retirement visa. Bank records should show a total of pension for the year at 800,000 through a combination of income, deposits and/or pension.

The individual granted the 90-day visa has to check in with any immigration office to give mention of your current address of residency in Thailand. This can also be done by mail, if, for any reason you are not able to personally go to the immigration office.

Alternatively, an individual can also hire the services of an agent who can carry out this task for you through power of attorney. It is common, available and very convenient.

Application Process

In order to be eligible to apply for Thai retirement visa, you would initially have to apply for a 90-day initial Non-Immigrant visa from your home country. Head over to the Thai embassy or consulate in your home country and start the process there. One in Thailand, enjoy your 60-day stay. Once you hit the last 30 days of your current permits validity, you may file your retirement visa application. Remember that in order to support your application you must have an updated bank book or passbook. These financial documents should be accompanied by a bank letter clearly stating that the money has been deposited to your bank account from a source overseas for not less than 2 months.

Visa Benefits

This visa allows an individual who wishes to make Thailand their long-term home away from home, a stay of up to one year. The individual on a retirement visa will also have the convenience of renewing their visa from within the country without having to go on a visa run.

The 1-year Non-Immigrant ED Visa or The Education Visa

The education visa, for all its perks and almost easy application process and approval, has (not surprisingly) been the most exploited form of Thai visa. It has been relentlessly exploited by many because of its long-term stay validity in the country. It was, and still is, also misused because there is a minimal financial commitment to the approval of the visa. All one would need to do is enroll in a language school and say you are staying to learn Thai and almost like magic, you get your brand-spanking new year-long-effective education visa.

When the Thai government got wind of that "students" were not really studying in Thailand to learn, they conducted a sting of sorts and ordered officers of the immigration to carry out random basic Thai language testing. These random Thai basic language tests were given to individuals who had reported to have been learning the language for several years. Many of these individuals, who took advantage of the lax requirements and the extended allowance to stay, got their educational visas revoked and cancelled. Should you want to take this route, make sure that you are showing up for your Thai classes at least twice a week, so as not to face embarrassment if called to have a random language exam.

Requirements

There are two ways for an individual who wants to apply for this visa to go about the process. One can either apply for an education visa in their country of origin by going to the nearest Thai embassy or consulate. Or you can go to Thailand on a tourist visa and locate a language school you will want to enroll with. Once enrolled with the language school, the task of sorting out your documents and paperwork for the visa will be worked out by the school with the Ministry of Education.

Any one of any nationality can apply for a 1-year Non-Immigrant Education visa. However there are some nationals who will have to apply for this in their home country. These are people from India, Iran, Sri Lanka, China, Bangladesh, China and nationals from Middle Eastern countries. If the school accepts your application for enrollment, and chances are high that you will be, the individual will have to exit the country and apply for the Non-Immigrant ED visa in any Thai embassy or consulate outside of Thailand.

When applying for an education visa in your home country, you will need to present the usual paperwork like your passport or your travel document showing its validity of no less than 6 months. The interested individual would also have to provide a recent 4 x 6 cm photograph of them.

On top of these, you will need to furnish a letter of acceptance from the language center you wish to study at. For individuals who want to study in a private institution, may be required to get an official letter from the Ministry of Education of Thailand or other sub-authorities concerned. The official letter from the Ministry of Education of Thailand is basically an approval of your enrollment along with a copy of the individual's registration certificate. Keep in mind that there are slight variations of the documents one would need to present as requirement for more specific fields of study and internships.

Application Process

If you are looking to spend time learning in Thailand whilst learning more about its rich culture and history, you would be glad to know that it is quite easy to apply for an education visa whilst in the country. Reason being is that language schools all over the country are looking to enroll more students and are therefore happy to oblige and do all the necessary work to enroll you and get your business. The only glitch in this seemingly almost-too-easy system is that the individual would have to head out to (usually) Laos or any of the nearer neighboring countries in the immediate region to obtain your education visa.

A returning individual on an education visa will be allowed to stay for 90 days upon their return to Thailand. Once school documents are furnished to you, this gives them the allowance to request for an extension every 90 days. The person on the student visa will need to head to the Bangkok Immigration Office for the length of their language course, which may take up to a maximum of 3 years. Each extension will carry a fee of 1, 900 baht.

Should a person, on a single entry ED visa want to travel overseas, they will have to first obtain a re-entry permit to in order for them to leave and come back into the country. Thankfully anyone intending to take a quick school break trip can conveniently get a re-entry permit at Suvarnabhumi Airport before getting on their flight. Make sure that you request a pause on your visa.

This effectively excludes the time spent away and will not be counted against the duration of the visa. To request for a permit to re-enter, make sure that you prepare your passport along with a copy of it, and one 4 x 6 cm passport photo. The fee for single entry is 1,000 baht, and 3,800 baht for multiple entries.

Visa Benefits

This visa will allow the individual continued stay in the country without having to go on a visa run every 90 days. This is not so for other sorts of Non Immigrant O visas. Although the individual holder of this visa will still have to report, every 90 days, to immigration, to update their address. You can wait up to a week before the due date to report, but do not forget this important requirement. Those on a single entry ED visa will also have to obtain a re-entry permit should they need or want to travel overseas. So, it makes better sense to get a multiple entry visa from the outset

The Marriage Visa Annexed to a Non Immigrant O Visa

Love is all around and you never know when Cupid aims his arrow at you and the significant other you are meant to be with. You could meet on a beach, at a bar, a cafe on the street. Or you may get to know each other online and decide to take it a step further and go the whole nine yards.

Marriage visas are tricky visas to understand for most countries in the world, and it is no different in Thailand. The Marriage Visa technically known as a 1-Year Extension of Stay Based on Marriage and there are a number of things to keep in mind in order to apply for one.

The first step is for the individual to apply for a 1-Year Non-Immigrant O visa or a 90-day visa at the Thai Embassy or Consulate in your home country or the country where you presently reside. An important bit of information to remember is that the 90-day Non-Immigrant visa can also be gotten from countries nearby Thailand.

The individual applying for the Non-Immigrant O visa will be doing so on the basis of being married to a Thai national so the interested individual will have to attach their marriage certificate and the copy of your husband's or wife's ID card along with their application for the visa. The Non-Immigrant O visa allows the individual a year's stay in Thailand under the condition that the person exits the country every 90 days. Follow the requirements below to extend your stay without having to leave.

Visa Requirements

For the married-to-a-local foreigner and Non-Immigrant O visa holder, getting an extension of the 1-year stay will require that you are married to a Thai local (national) and that you have no bad record with the law (no criminal history). The individual should also have a monthly income of at least 40,000 Baht, or a Thai bank account with 400,000 Baht for two months.

Here is the official law about the financial requirements to meet the 400k money-in-the-bank requirement:

- A foreigner wed to a Thai woman; the alien husband will have to bring home an annual income of an average of and no less than 40,000 baht each month, or he should have no less than 400,000 baht in a Thailand bank account for the past two months in order to cover living expenses for a year.

This visa is renewable every year and this process can be carried out whilst inside Thailand. The paperwork needed to get the visa is pretty straight forward and the same as when the individual initially received it. There is also a requirement for the marriage visa holder to report to the nearest immigration office every 90 days within the vicinity of your area of residence to update your current address.

Keep in mind that should the individual need to travel outside of Thailand after getting the marriage visa; the individual will require a re-entry permit to travel overseas. Forgetting to get one will cancel the visa you hold upon your exit from the country. The Non-Immigrant O visa re-entry permit can be applied for at the nearest immigration office or at any Thai international airport. Do this before leaving the country. Keep in mind that this does not apply to the 1-year multiple entries visa but is applicable to the visa which was extended in Thailand for the period of 12 months.

Application Process

The process of getting a Non Immigrant O visa based on marriage is a straightforward process which begins with the interested individual applying for one in your home country. Simply furnish a translated copy of you and your spouse's marriage certificate along with a copy of your wife's/husband's identification card. When you have gotten the multiple entries, Non-Immigrant O visa, all you will need to do next is travel to Thailand to get the visa activated.

The 1-year extension can be applied for on the last 30 days of your 90-day permit to stay, given that you meet the financial requirements mentioned earlier. It usually takes about a month to process this. The one-year extension is not mandatory, but a convenience. If the individual does not want to do this, they could merely exit the country every 90 days.

Visa Benefits

Once the individual has obtained their marriage visa, which is an extended Non Immigrant O based on marriage, they will have the convenience of staying in Thailand for a whole year without the hassle and expense of going on a visa run. The individual holding this sort of visa will also be able to get employment in the country as long as they are able to get a valid Thai work permit which can be presented side by side with your marriage visa. All this together, not only allows the individual to stay in the country legally, but work there legally, as well.

The Thailand Elite Visa

The Thailand Elite Visa is a multiple entry visa, valid for five years, and renewable as long as the membership is still valid. With the basic package starting at a cool 500,000 Baht, you will be granted a 1-year stay, with an extension possible at the end of the year. With that said, getting the Thailand Elite Visa, if you have the finances for it, is the simplest method of how one will be able to reside in Thailand on a long term basis and it comes with additional perks that make the holder a tad bit special.

This visa is a multiple entry visa that will be valid for five years upon receipt and is able to be renewed as long as the visa is still effective. The Thailand Elite visa lives up to its name with a whopping 500, 000 baht. This fee allows you a guaranteed stay in the country for a year, with the possibility of extending it at the end of the year. We've compiled the proper information for you here to save you the time of the confusing business of complicated translating.

Requirements

There are two important requirements for the interested individual to meet for the Thailand Elite visa. One is that they have the funds for the visa and the second is that the individual is not banned from or found to have a criminal record the country.

Visa Benefits

The foreign individual who is a Thailand Elite Visa holder need not go on those pesky visa runs, but will still have to report every 90 - day to update immigration with their most current residence address. And even this will not pose a problem on your time since you will have a personal Thai Elite liaison officer to handle this for you. Additional perks, aside from the timely renewal of your visa with no hassle on your part, is a concierge service that will be waiting for you at the airport. You are greeted and ushered into a limo and driven to your hotel. The holders of this visa get spa treatments, a medical checkup, and get to enjoy discount shopping in the country. They also enjoy cheaper banking with Bangkok Bank and a plethora of other little gift and perk bits that you may or may not use.

Rules on Overstaying

Do not make the mistake of overstaying your welcome in Thailand. Be sure to have a look at either the length of your permit by stamp or your particular visa to see what date it is you are supposed to leave Thailand. You are considered to be overstaying even if your visa ended the previous day.

Overstaying your welcome in Thailand could get you into serious trouble, so make it a point that you have a big calendar and your smart phone to remind you of the nearing due date. To ensure that you are aware of the clauses of your visa, make sure to look at the duration of the permit given to you (either the stamp or the particular visa you hold) to check the date that you are supposed to leave Thailand. If you miss one day after the due date you would have already overstayed.

In the past, the overstaying offender would be slapped with a 500 baht fine for each day they are in the country outside of the visa validity. This penalty has now been increased to not just the 500 baht fine but with an entry ban from the country for severe offenders. As of March 2016, one could be banned from Thailand for as long as 10 years. An overstaying individual who turns themselves in will be banned from the country for a year, if they overstayed for more than 90 days. A person who overstays their welcome for more than a year will be banned from entering the country for three years.

Those who overstay for three years will not be allowed back into the country for a length of five years, and the individual found to be staying in the country for over five years will not be given entry to the country for the next 10 years. Be mindful of the expiration date of your visa because as much as Thailand is known to be the country of smiles and happy people, you will be given the proper "punishment" for disobeying a law. Make sure that you extend your visa and apply for the proper permission to stay at the Office of Immigration Bureau, located on Government Center B, Chaengwattana Soi 7, Laksi, Bangkok 10210, Tel 0-2141-9889.

Visa extension & Re-entry permit

Non-immigrant visas are valid for 90 days upon entry to the country. Make sure that you have these scheduled and sorted out before the expiry date in order for you and your spouse to get a year-long visa extension. Non-immigrant O visas for children, accompanied by their parents, will and can only be extended until the dependent is 20 years old. Upon reaching the age of 20, he/she must apply for a Thai visa on his/her own merit. To get this process done would mean that child may be signed up at a local university, which would make them eligible for an ED visa or duly employed, therefore have a work permit, allowing them a stipulated period of residence in the country.

Chapter Six: Square Away Your Finances

Heading out to start a new chapter of your life, no matter where the location is, takes research planning and time. If you are given that luxury of being able to sort out your business, taking the time to understand the ins and outs of the financial scene of the country you are moving to enables you to keep your spending power. Your ability to set aside your finances will be an important aspect you want to square away immediately as these take time and meticulous study.

You wouldn't want to end up in a country where you are not able to access your money as you once did because of the differing banking laws of each country. Going down to street-level, everyday banking, not sorting out your finances, could leave you with low cash and a headache of a time trying to access your overseas accounts.

It can be easy to get carried away spending cash you know you have in this country (which seems to sparkle under the sun, being that Thailand has some of the best finds and buys that are definitely quite unique compared to the stuff you are used to seeing and having in your home city. You just never want to go overboard during your initial year here, however tempting it can be to spend cash faster than it comes in. Sure, your home country currency may have a lot more spending power here, but if you are not earning that same sort of money on a regular basis, whatever on-hand, available finances you have stashed away will trickle like a dripping faucet soon enough.

Everyone says that living in most of the Asian countries like, Vietnam, Thailand or the Philippines is cheap, but this isn't really so, unless you live like a local in whichever country you may find yourself. If you start looking for the comforts and trappings of home, you may soon find yourself spending considerably more than if you were home. It is true that South-East Asian economies are generally far cheaper compared to Western countries. Hostels can go for as little as $3-5 a night, and meals can cost as low as $0.50-$1.

Online hotel booking sites have promotions and discounts that shave off a considerable chunk off room rates as compared to just simply popping in front of a hotel receptionist to ask for a room. Best of all, flying to Bangkok could cost you as little as $500 from most airports of the world. With more and more airlines working hand in hand, airfares have become a lot cheaper than they have ever been and it is so much more possible for many to fly.

As with most developing and developed countries of the world, the cost of living in Thailand will greatly depend on the area of the country you ultimately decide to stay. This would not only hinge largely on the type and quality of life you expect but the manner in which you are accustomed. This is especially so if you can't do without the cheese, wine, cured meats, beers and imported foods from your home country. These would definitely cost a premium getting them locally. Locally made clothes can be a bargain and there are places where you can find some pretty affordable clothes fit for the weather, but this is a whole different challenge if you are a tall person looking for sizes and the brands you would normally get in your home port.

Open a Thai Bank Account

Make it a point to get this one off your list over the first few weeks of your stay in Thailand. Doing so will save you the exorbitant withdrawal fees when using your home bank cards. It also saves you time from ATMs not accepting your home bank cards at the most inopportune of times, like on a night out or when short on cash at the local convenience store. You may have to scout around for the bank that will extend you the services you will need but there are definitely banks that can accommodate the type of banking needs you require.

You may be surprised by the different documents required at each local bank in order for you to open an account in a Thai bank. Even more frustratingly, many of the bank staff would have minimal to no knowledge of the regulations stipulated on bank websites. You may want to look for the head of the bank to speak to or the one who speaks English the best in order to get the business of inquiries squared away. Many expats who come to Thailand and attempt to open a bank account find it a struggle to have to deal with statements from bank staff who says that rules have changed since that posting or that the bank manager says otherwise.

Banks in Thailand

Life would be a heck of a lot easier for you when you have a Thai bank account with an ATM card. Not only would you be able to transfer money conveniently, you would also have the convenience of access to funds as long as there are working cash machines in the area. However, no matter what sort of visa holder you may be, opening an account can be a massive headache and confounding! There have been many instances when people on tourist visas got to open bank accounts faster and hassle-free than individuals who are holders of marriage, retirement, work permit or Non O visa. Therefore, to save you the hassle of trudging the humid city pavements after doing your Internet research, we've compiled a list of banks others have found success and are happily maintaining Thai bank accounts today.

Kasikorn Bank

Commonly known as K-Bank, this bank is suitable for Individuals who have base in foreign countries. You would need to present your passport, work permit or education visa. However, do not be surprised if these are not required at every branch. Most times the minimum requirements would get you an account on the spot with an accompanying debit card issued to you.

UOB Bank

This bank is suitable for an Individual Non-Resident Account. You would be required to present a copy of your passport, a copy of your work permit, although this depends largely on the branch and is not always required. You would also be required to put up a 50,000 baht deposit as well as your phone number. .Most times the minimum requirements would get you an account on the spot with an accompanying debit card issued to you.

CitiBank

The requirements of CitiBank would include a copy of both your passport and work permit or a minimum 1-year apartment contract. The minimum requirements would get you an account going for you immediately after transaction.

SCB

The requirements of SCB as of 2017 would be that the individual present a work permit. Non-resident accounts are suitable for tourists and foreign visitors of the country, foreigners working temporarily in Thailand, foreign government agencies such as embassies and consulates, including specialized UN agencies like UNICEF, FAO, ESCAP, etc.

Bangkok Bank

The bank requirements one will need to present would be their passport along with one other official identification document like, a certified letter from your Embassy, stating that you have duly presented your passport to your Embassy, and that the embassy acknowledge that this is indeed your passport. Depending on the Embassy, you will have to pay a fee for this certified letter costing anywhere between 1150-1750 baht. Aside from the certified letter from your Embassy other documents you may need to present is a letter from your home bank or a personage acceptable to the bank. You will also have to furnish the bank with evidence of your address in Thailand as well as your regular address in your home country.

Credit Cards

You know that old credit card commercial reminding you to not leave home without it? Well don't, since Credit cards are widely used in Bangkok and other major cities of Thailand. Most major credit cards e.g. American Express, MasterCard, VISA, Diners Club, etc., are accepted in Thailand.

For American Express, you can either visit their office or call them at 0-2273-5500. Alternatively, one can also apply for MasterCard and VISA at most major local and international bank branches. However, requirements may vary from bank to bank. The following documentation listed below should typically be provided to the bank along with the completed application form:

- A copy of your passport

- A copy of your work permit

- A copy of your bank account details for the preceding two to six month period (the requirement varies with each bank)

- A recent salary statement or a certificate of income

Be aware that it can be a tad more difficult for an expat to apply for a credit card and would likely have to show proof of long term employment with a more than sufficient (higher) income to cover for any credit extended. There are banks which require a minimum of Baht 25,000, though some banks, for example, Kasikorn Bank would require a minimum of 50,000 baht to get approved.

One suggestion we can give is the much easier option of bypassing banks and applying for a Visa or MasterCard at a reputable store such as Central. The process of application is similar but they are likelier to grant you the card.

Payment Services

Bill payments can be conveniently paid through banks, ATM machines, 7-Eleven stores and select supermarkets. Pay@Post is an online bill payment service available at all branches of the post office. Fees may vary.

Chapter Seven: Long – Term Living

Get to know that many living options available to you in Thailand, especially if you are planning on planting roots in any country. Thailand is no different in that aspect but can be quite different from the living conditions you are currently accustomed to in your home country. Most Thai abodes are no bigger than a one-room deal, often lacking in amenities and utilities. You don't get much, costing around $15 a month and these places are not typically up for lease.

Another option you could look into is a cheap hostel, where you can plunk your bag and your head for about $100. For this amount of money, you get a bed in a room that you will be sharing with other people. This could have a kitchen or it may not. If you are comfortable sharing a room with other people but can't do without a room to cook food, then scouting around for a hostel with one would be something you would need to figure out. The likelihood for the hostel to have hot running water is also slim to none. You could probably find an austere condo for the same price if you are particular about privacy.

Other perks you can take advantage of, should you be a work permit holder, a long-stay visa holder or a permanent resident is a wider range of banking services. Under these visas and on the conditions of your permanent residency status, you would be able to get a cheque account, online international funds services as well as internet banking.

Tourist areas like Phuket, Koh Samui and the likes are understandably places that you will need to be financially ready for when you visit. However, in terms of long term residency, Central Bangkok, just like most big cities and capitals in the world, is the most expensive area of Thailand. However, even island life can be economical if you do your homework about places to stay and eateries with delicious local fare that doesn't break the bank each time you get a hankering. That being said this is where the line is drawn and contrast between vacationing and residing in Thailand becomes apparent. The longer one lives in the country, the better they become accustomed to the real become part of the community. You get the feel of the actual local prices.

Accommodation

It is not difficult to find a place to rent in Bangkok with western style accommodations. There are countless condominiums, Apartments and houses in the area which you can lease. Common accommodations for an expatriate would be a condo or apartment located in the center of the city or conveniently along the BTS-MRT lines. Apartment and condo units range from 45 sq. meters to 250 square meters. There are choices of studio apartments to one to three en-suite bedrooms. Some of these places even have amenities such as a fitness gym and/or a swimming pool.

The main types of accommodation are categorized as either, serviced apartments, condominiums and individual houses. Let's look at each type of accommodation typical to the expat in Thailand.

Serviced Apartments

Serviced apartments are owned by a company, and these apartments are usually fully furnished so this saves you the hassle of having to shop for furniture and kitchen tools, wares, and gadgets. Serviced apartments are typically equipped and come complete with a TV, a refrigerator, beddings, crockery, a kettle and or a microwave.

The amount you pay for rent will usually be inclusive of apartment cleaning services, such as changing bed linen, maintenance of the toilet and bath, etc. Laundry services would typically also be available in many serviced apartments. A short menu of available food from the serviced apartment is often available for room service meals.

The advantages to living in a serviced apartment is the on-site staff who, if not on call, can do your bidding with no need for you to employ a maid. All you need is to bring your clothes, toiletries and personal effects and you're all set! The convenience of living in a serviced apartment are many with all utility bills paid to one entity and is much like living in a hotel.

There are some disadvantages like having no control over the maids visiting over and praying there are some disadvantages like having no control over the maids visiting or Entering your room. Petty theft is a common complaint, and Utility bills, such as electricity, phone and water charges are much higher than if you were living in a regular apartment.

Housing compounds and Non-serviced apartments

These residential units are usually owned by one company or family. These apartments or houses are not serviced and you can either get a maid to do the job of cleaning for you or you can save and do it yourself.

These Apartments are rented out furnished, partially furnished or unfurnished housing compounds not as common as apartments. However, you pay for the advantage of on-site maintenance, with staff usually available 24 hours a day. Common area is the responsibility of a single landlord, which usually results in good maintenance, cleaning, etc.

Another convenience is that all bills are payable to the one entity and tenants have more control over who has access to their apartment. There have been reports of landlords padding utility bills.

Condominiums

These units are generally owned and managed by separate and individual landlords. You can lease a condominium which can either furnish or unfurnished. There are varied standards. You can find good deals on condominiums if you know where to look. The standard utility charges of a condo unit are billed directly to you. From the telephone, water and electric bills, etc., all these are billed at standard rates. The renter has more control over who can come and go into your unit and you may find it easier to change telephone service providers, should you wish.

Condominiums tend to be more individual in furnishings. As with other places, there are some disadvantages that you may have to deal with, but finding the right landlord will be heaven-sent. Some landlords less than upstanding and there have been reports of difficulty recovering your deposit. In some cases, condo units may have a low occupancy rate and under these circumstances, it is typical for cost-cutting measures to be administered.

When this is the circumstance you may notice a reduction in security of the building, cleaning and maintenance of common areas may be lackluster, lighting, pest control may not be up to par. It is less common for a condo to have an o-site English speaking staff.

Independent Houses

Independent houses are perfect choices for small families because there are many available detached and terraced houses in and around the city which can be rented from individual landlords. These houses are typically cheaper than residences in a compound. However, there are no security services and the tenant would have to be responsible for their own security. It is also unlikely for an individual house to provide an on-site staff when you need assistance for repairs, etc., but you can most likely call your landlord and set up an appointment for any repairs or replacements you need done. Independent housing seems to be a more popular choice amongst expats who have had some experience of living in Bangkok. These houses usually cost lower in rent than the previous two choices mentioned above with more individual style housing to choose from. They are often quaint, very picturesque and Thai in style, decor, furnishings and design. Individual housing can be found in city centre. You enjoy a higher level of privacy as well.

Choosing Your Neighborhood

Expats tend to choose locations that are populated and near train lines although many have also been here long enough to understand the ins and outs of living in Thailand giving them the confidence to branch further into the fringes of the city and still get around fairly comfortably. Still, the most sought after locations of expats living in Thailand are the Central Bangkok area, Nichada Thani, Lakeside Bang-Na, and along the BTS - MRT route.

Central Bangkok

Central Bangkok or known as the Sukhumvit/Sathorn areas are some the major business districts of Bangkok. A large choice of apartment style flats is available at various prices. These apartments are more convenient to the new expat since they are closer in proximity to the hub and centre of Bangkok. Finding an apartment here would mean that you are nearer to restaurants,, malls, department stores, the BTS, and most offices. This location can be ideal for a family with children relocating to the city of Bangkok since they would be closer to the Shrewsbury International School, and the New International School of Thailand, to mention some.

Nichada Thani

This area of has lauded itself to be the expatriate town of Thailand. With a housing compound which consists of over 800 housing units and located on the northern outskirts of the city, this gated community offers the conveniences of living within the general area of the city with the conveniences of having a supermarket, a Starbucks, stores, and fitness gyms not too far away. Nichada Thani is located near the International School of Bangkok and the Harrow International School, to mention a few. The Nichada Thani compound is known as Thailand's first planned community. The community consists of top-level detached homes. There are many units with their own pools. There is a clubhouse and a lake not too far off. Check out this website for additional information: www.nichada.com.

You would also be able to find additional choices of expat housing compounds around the Nichada locale which are close to the close to Don Mueang Airport

Lakeside Villas Bang-Na

If you prefer living in a smaller community compound then you will be glad to know that there is a slightly smaller cluster of expat housing to the South East of the city. The Lakeside Villas of Bang-Na is a convenient area because it is near the Bangkok Pattana International School. Indicative of its name, the housing compounds of the Lakeside Villas in Bang-Na are surrounded by lakes, making for a picturesque landscape and perfect for the jogger in you. These are gated communities and boast of several convenient facilities, like a clubhouse and communal swimming pool.

Easy access from the compounds is several superstores and big department stores like the only IKEA in Thailand, the Mega Bangna, and the Central Bangna. And with the airport a mere twenty minutes away, the convenience of small community living is made easier and more accessible.

Along BTS-MRT Route

The convenience of the extended operating route of the BTS and MRT, covering a greater area and distance of the city make living conditions a tad easier for the expat, hence many are drawn to find housing along the BTS-MRT route. Here, tenants have the convenient access to the lines that go into and through the city, making commuting to work easier. Because of the easy access to transportation system, many expats choose to live here, especially those who work in the city and need the easy access of convenient and affordable transportation.

Restrictions on Land Ownership for Foreigners

Who wouldn't want a little piece of paradise to return to or a second home away from home, where they can fly off to during cold winter months? Having a taste of calling Thailand your nest away from your usual digs is enough to get anyone thinking about getting property to come back to on a regular basis. The beauty of the land and the magnificence of its culture and people are enough to conjure images of coming home to languish in balmy beaches, and being part of a bustling cityscape. Now, depending on the sort of property you wish to acquire, like a house or a condo unit, you will have to keep in mind that there are a number of restrictions on the kind of property a foreigner can buy but the good news is, it could be possible.

By general rule, with a small possibility several exceptions, foreigners are restricted from buying land and property in Thailand. The exceptions of ownership apply to owning land for the purposes of commercial usage rather than residential. On top of the restrictions, the conveyance system in Thailand is pretty unique and confounding. In order to determine whether a foreigner will be allowed to acquire property, and even more importantly, if the links of the title of the potential property is valid would need the aid of expert legal and professional advice.

Buying a condominium is a procedure that is more straightforward and has fewer restrictions. However, there are still imposed requirements for the foreigner looking into purchasing a condo. The bright side is that these imposed requirements are not as prohibitive, making it possible for the interested individual to make it happen. One of the most important requirements that an interested condo buyer may have to present is evidence that the acquisition was closed using a specific amount of foreign currency brought into Thailand.

Another method of having some sort of long-term "ownership" is by lease of a property. A foreign national will be able to lease an area of land or a house for up to 30 years. After this 30 year lease is up, the lessor will have an option to renew the lease for another 30 year period. This agreement is called the 2x30 option. The individual may erect a residential building on the leased land. Leases that go beyond 3 years have to be registered against the title of the property and it will be up to the lessor to pay taxes on the lease amount of the property on a scheduled basis.

Chapter Eight: Settling In

Living in Thailand has enriched the lives of many who have chosen to call this beautiful country of smiles home. Setting yourself up for success integration into the country and community of your choosing would mean that you would need to do the initial necessary work of researching everything you need to know before you move there. Faux pas are excusable for the transient tourist and is usually met with a snicker and tolerance. Not so for the individual intending to call Thailand their new home.

Let's look at some of the common practices and customs the local residents and native of Thailand, so that you get yourself and your family up to speed about what to do, and what to expect when the actual move happens.

Working in Thailand

If your intention is to work in the Land of Smiles, you will need to obtain a work permit in addition to obtaining a visa. An expat who holds down a job in Thailand is also obligated to obtain a work permit before they start working in the country. Applicants to job openings must be a holder of a non-immigrant visa, category B, in order to be given a work permit and begin working in Thailand.

Foreigners employed in Thailand are subject to the Alien Employment Act (B.E.2521). Under the provisions of this Act, any foreigner cannot perform any sort of act of work or service unless a work permit has been issued by the Employment Department, or the individual or the work performed falls within an exception to the Act.

Here are six categories of foreigners who are exempted from work permit requirements:

- Those who are members of the diplomatic corps, or a consular mission.

- Those who are representatives of member countries or officials of the United Nations and all its specialized agencies.

- All personal domestic servants hailing from another country to work for persons under the individuals mentioned above on a regular basis.

- All persons who perform any duties or missions in the Kingdom under arrangement between the government of Thailand and a foreign government or an international organization.

- All persons given permission by the government of Thailand to enter in order to perform any duties or mission in the Kingdom.

- All persons who perform duties for the benefit of education, culture, arts, sport or such other activities as prescribed by Royal Decree.

The term "work" is broadly defined as "working by exerting one's physical energy or employing one's knowledge, whether or not for wages or other benefits". So, a foreign housewife of an expat doing volunteer or charity work would theoretically have to have a work permit for her to continue with her volunteer or charity outreach.

However, if absolutely necessary, one can apply for an urgent work permit should the individual be entering Thailand for a short period of time so as to perform "urgent and essential work". This is for a period that is no longer than 15 days. Take note that the following is stipulated to be urgent and essential work:

Administrative and educational works the following:

- **Conference, discussion, seminar or business invitation works**

  o Temporary internal audit

  o Special lecture and educational work

  o Aviation superintendent work

- **Technical work**

  o Inspection, follow-up and technical solution works

  o Meeting work on machinery installation and technique

  o Aircraft engineering work, aircraft mechanical work

  o Machine repairing or installing work

  o Petroleum technical work

  o Mechanical demonstrative or testing work

  o Technical training and seminar work

- Movie taking work

- **Overseas recruitment work**

  - Worker screening work

  - Skill testing work

- **Miscellaneous work**

  - Purchasing work

  - Tour liaison

  - Public contribution work which is of non-commercial or non-profit objectives

Jobs and tasks which the director-general or the officer authorized by the director-general shall deem appropriate to accept special notifications upon interim necessity.

A person who needs to obtain a work permit will have two main avenues they could take where which work permits may be sought. These namely are at a One Stop Service Centre, or the Ministry of Labour

- The One Stop Service Centre is an office set up to expedite the handling of applications for work permits from employers who fit a specific bill and meet certain criteria. When the possibility of going this route, the Service Centre can normally approve a work permit application on the day of submission.

When the individual or the employer do not fit the bill of the criteria of utilizing the services of the One Stop Service Centre, work permits will have to be sought from the Ministry of Labor. Necessary visas, on the other hand, can be sought from the Immigration Bureau.

- A work permit will look like a passport-sized booklet showing details of where the individual is allowed to work, the job description, etc.

Should there be any changes to these particulars; the individual should immediately contact their immigration service provider. Working in a location or for a position not detailed in the work permit is not definitely something you would not want to do.

There are 39 jobs which only Thais can perform and are not permitted to be carried out foreigners. These are mainly:

- manual and industrial labor

- work in agriculture

- animal breeding

- forestry

- fishery and farm supervision

- carpentry

- shop assistant jobs

- accountancy positions

- hairdresser jobs

- civil engineering positions

- legal services

- architectural work

- dressmaking tasks

- clerical or secretarial work amongst others.

Visa and Work Permit Cancellation

Get in touch with the Immigration Bureau to cancel out your visa at the end of your assignment. Law does not require you to cancel your work permit because it will automatically expire and lose its validity. Immigration law in Thailand is a complex issue. Seek out professional advice regarding these matters on a regular basis.

Tax Structure and Liability as a Taxpayer

Although not particularly sophisticated, Thai personal income tax legislation, is relatively all-encompassing, and states:

- All earned income coming from a Thai employment is subject to Thai personal income tax. This is whether or not the recipient is resident, or of where in Thailand the income is paid.

- A resident individual is also subject to Thai personal income tax on any foreign source of income if the income is remitted to Thailand.

- An individual who spends 180 consecutive days (or more) in Thailand in a calendar year, shall will be classified as a resident of Thailand for the purposes income tax.

Take note that the Thai tax year follows the calendar year and earned income which is taxable would include, but not limited to the following:

- Salary, wages, etc.

- Per diems

- Any received bonus

- Pensions and commissions

- Personal income tax paid by an employer

- Accommodation costs paid by an employer

- Capital gains are taxable as part of an individual's income.

Capital losses incurred are not deductible from one's personal income. There are specific available tax exemptions in regard of gains earned on Thai Stock Exchange Securities, and exemptions on some immovable property, such as real estate.

- Foreign currency –Income received in foreign (i.e. non-Thai) currency, for tax purposes shall converted into Thai Baht in respect to the exchange rate in force on the day of receipt.

Heads up, married couples! Since the 2012 tax year, the income of a wife has no longer been treated or considered as the income of her husband. Therefore, a husband and wife who both earn a living can choose to file their income tax returns jointly or separately.

Tax Returns

Individuals who live in Thailand are subject to file their annual income tax return by the end of March stating the income they received during the previous year. This mandate comes with very few exceptions.

A non-working spouse is not be subject to turn in an annual tax return. But, should an individual gain income from the list itemized below, they would be subject to turn in the tax return of the first half-year by the end of September of the year wherein they received the income. They should also file their annual tax return in order to report the full year income of the individual by the end of March, the following year. Tax paid in the first half-year, if applicable, shall be credited against their annual tax.

Hiring Property

- Liberal professions (law, medicine, engineering architecture, accountancy, and fine arts)

- A contract to which a contractor provides essential construction materials excluding tools

- Carrying on commercial or industrial businesses i.e. trading and services

Payments

Income tax due on earnings from a Thai employer must be withheld at the source by the employer. All other taxes due must be paid simultaneously when the tax return is handed in to the authorities. Tax due amounts of at least 3,000 baht may be paid in three equal installments. The first installment is to paid upon filing the return; the second and the third installments are each paid one month after the previous payment has been satisfied.

Hiring Domestic Help

A perk most westerner's find, living in Thailand, is the availability of hiring house help and the quality of the service they get from the hired help. Not to mention the low cost of the expected salary. However, there are enough stories to fill volumes of books regarding the experiences of domestic staff in Thailand. Make it a point to consider the following pointers we will be laying out for you with regard to hiring house help.

- The most common chores you would expect a maid under your employment would include house cleaning chores, the laundry, tending to a garden, and shopping for grocery. Expect to pay a premium salary for domestic help with good cooking skills. You will not have to pay as if you had a personal chef on your payroll, but they will charge a higher price for the skills they bring to the household. Range of salary will depend largely on the location of the family, number of people in the household, the duties to be handled, and if you require a maid to understand English. Maids expect to be paid in cash on a monthly or bi-monthly basis. It will be up to you and the potential maid to make that agreement.

• Hired help are frequently hired on a basis of them living with the family, so consider your dwelling and figure out if you have the space or if you are comfortable about having a non-family member living with you. You may also make arrangements for the maid to work for you on a day to day basis, with specific work hours. Make this absolutely clear during the interview and determine whether both you and the maid agree on a live-in or daily work basis. Should they be agreeable to a live in agreement, keep in mind that you will either have to provide for their food or give them a monthly stipend for meal allowance. They will have to cook their own food and take space for the food supplies they will need, so consider these as well.

- An English speaking maid who will be taking charge of cleaning, ironing and cooking will cost about 10,000 baht a month and expects payment on a monthly basis. Again, clarify this with the potential help. Keep in mind that you will also have to consider the monthly overhead additional in terms of food. Determine the monthly food allowance you will both agree upon, or whether you will be providing for their food.

- It is not unusual for an expat, especially one with a family, to have a driver on the payroll. The driver will usually be responsible for driving the family around, delivering or collecting packages, like dry cleaning, accompanying the maid on her grocery shopping duties for the family, car cleaning and taking care of getting the car maintained and fixed when needed.

- Most skilled and English speaking maids are foreign maids who come from Burma or the Philippines. This is due to the supposed higher ability of maids, from these countries, of speaking English. They will be required to get work permits. Getting a maid locally or from nearby Laos, Cambodia or Burma, is usually the most advisable and easier to arrange. Any other nationality employed by you will have to go to the proper process of obtaining a work visa. If a foreign maid is working for you and you did not arrange for their services and work on their work permit, they may be working in Thailand illegally.

- Make sure that the maids you interview provide evidence of previous work experience and present a couple of solid references from previous employers, which you can check.

- It is more than a good idea to draw up a contract between you and the help you hire, whether a driver or a maid, clearly stating the hours of work expected to be given, and in some cases, what encompasses their employment duties as well as the probationary period which shouldn't go beyond 120 days.

- Nannies and maids given childcare duties will definitely require a higher salary. Make this clear, if this is the sort of services you would require of the domestic help you are employing.

- Maids are covered by labor law rights and are entitled to a full severance pay.

- Asian maids, unless formerly employed and trained by a western employer will not know how to handle winter wear. So make sure that you either train the maid on handling them, or you take care of them yourself.

- Require that the maid/ driver furnish you a copy of her/his identification card upon contract signing of employment.

Medical Care

Hospitals

Finding out where to get the proper medical care, especially for families with children or who have members who would need medical attention or maintenance. You'd be glad to know that there are a number of relatively high standard hospitals available in Bangkok.

There are more than several public and private hospitals staffed by physicians who are internationally qualified. Private hospitals, in particular, are equipped with modern medical technology.

You need not make an appointment for the first visit to a hospital or clinic, but any succeeding visit with a specialist will require you to call in in advance. Make sure that you ask about the doctor's schedule. We've compiled a list of reputable hospitals below for your convenience:

Bangkok Hospital

2 Soi Soonvijai 7, New Petchburi Rd.,

Bangapi, Huay Kwang Bangkok 10310

Tel. 02-310-3000, 1719

www.bangkokhospital.com

BNH (or Bangkok Nursing Home Hospital)

9/1 Convent Rd., Silom, Bangkok 10500

Tel. 0-2686-2700

www.bnhhospital.com

Bumrungrad Hospital

33 Sukhumvit 3 (Soi Nana Nua),

Wattana, Bangkok 10110

Tel. 0-2667-1000, 0-2667-1000 (for emergency)

www.bumrungrad.com

Kasemrad Hospital

950 Prachachuen Rd., Bangsue, Bangkok 10800

Tel. 0-2910-1600

www.kasemrad.co.th

Mission Hospital

430 Pitsanuloke Rd., Siyak Mahanak,

Dusit, Bangkok 10300

Tel. 0-2282-1100, 0-2667-2999 (for emergency)

www.mission-hospital.org

Samitivej Hospital

133 Sukhumvit 49, Klongton Nua,

Wattana, Bangkok 10110

Tel. 0-2711-8181

www.samitivejhospitals.com

Medical Insurance

There are several international medical insurance providers which hold forth in Thailand. Make sure that you get in touch with your health insurance provider for their contact numbers and address in Thailand, should they be operating there.

BUPA Blue Cross

38 Q House Convent Building, Convent Rd.,

Silom, Bangrak, Bangkok 10500

Tel. 0-2677-0000

www.bupa.co.th

Krungthai Axa Life Insurance

2034/116-123, 136-143 ItalThai Tower,

New Petchburi Rd., Bang Kapi, Huay Khwang, Bangkok 10310

Tel. 0-2689-4800, 0-2723-4000

www.krungthai-axa.co.th

LMG Insurance

2 Sukhumvit 23, Lhlongtoey Nua,

Wattana Bangkok 10110

Tel. 0-2661-6000

www.lmginsurance.co.th

Manulife Insurance

364/30 Sri Ayudaya Rd., Phayathai,

Ratewi, Bangkok 10400

Tel. 0-2246-7650

www.manulife.co.th

Thai Health Insurance Plc.

121/89 RS Tower Bldg, 31st Fl.,

Ratchadapisek Rd., Dindaeng, Bangkok 10400

Tel. 0-2202-9200

www.thaihealth.co.th

Should the company you work for not provide healthcare coverage for you or your family members, there are local medical insurers who may be able to assist you.

Mobile Phones, 3G and Internet Services

It was only recently when 3G services of the international standard of 2.1-gigahertz frequency became available in Thailand. The country's three largest operators are AIS, DTAC and TrueMove. These telcos began providing new 3G services earlier in May 2013.

Each network provider offers different data plans at different rates and this goes for calling and texting services as well. Each 3g provider has a slight variation of signal strength and network coverage. Make sure to check out promotions from all of the operators to find which one would best suit your needs. With the EMI system disabled, one can now change phone service providers without having to get a new phone, as long as your phone uses the same system. Opting to acquiring a registered Thai mobile phone would entail a contract and you would need to provide the following documents:

- Original and copy of passport
- Original work permit
- Letter from employer (not over 3-months old)

Alternatively acquisition of a mobile phone with a prepaid option could be another choice to consider. However, the international roaming service coverage would be limited. To get a list of countries where international roaming service is available, check out the Call Centre numbers listed below.

- **DTAC**

  Call Centre 1678, 0-2202-7000

  www.dtac.co.th

- **AIS**

  Call Centre 1175, 0-2271-9000

  www.ais.co.th

Chapter Nine: Transportation and Getting Around

Located within the arrival hall behind the customs checkpoint is service counters offering transportation services for your convenient entry to the city proper. You will be taking your chances and might pay more than the premium price for a speeding, dinky cab gotten off the line of the airport taxi line. However, there are metered taxis to take your chances with outside the airport doors.

Just expect that you may a bit higher for the trip into the city. Most of the time, finding an English speaking taxi driver will be a challenge. If you are patient enough, you will find one who will be happy to do his job. You could also get the services of an airport limousine instead of booking two cabs for a bigger party with more baggage to lug. There are car rental booths that you can approach for a rental, if you prefer driving.

Airport Limousine

Offering a massive fleet of air-conditioned, chauffeured limousines and minibuses both are two transport service companies the Thai Limousine Services (operated by Thai Airways International) and the AOT Limousine Services (run by the Airports of Thailand). Found at the airport counters are reservation agents who can answer your questions in English and take care of booking your journey.

Thai Limousine Services

Fare: To downtown starting from Baht 1,500

Tel: 0-2308-8399 or book online at

www.thailimousinecenter.com

AOT Limousine Services

Counter: Service Counters are located on the 2nd

floor at Baggage Claims and Arrival Hall

exits, channel A, B and C.

Fare: To downtown starting from Baht 500

Tel: 0-2134-2323-5

Taxi

Public taxis are commonly used for commuting from
the airport. However, if you're new to Thailand, it is possible
that a taxi driver may take you for a lengthier ride in order
to earn extra money. The good news is if you get your phone
set up for 3G Internet services, you will be able to use your

map app to show the shortest route to your destination. The taxi stand can be located at the Platform of Passenger Terminal on the 1st floor, Gate 4 and 7. The fare is based on meter plus 50 baht surcharge from airport, plus expressway fees Tel: 0-2132-9199

Airport Rail Link

A good way to avoid gridlock and being tossed around inside a public Thai cab (they would give the drivers of the F&F franchise a run for their money) would be the Airport Rail Link train system consists of two service routes as follows,

SA City Line

The City line (blue line) operates between the terminals of Suvarnabhumi Airport and the Phaya Thai station. The train stops at 6 stations along the way: Lat Krabang, Ban Thap Chang, Hua Mak, Ramkhamhaeng, Makkasan and Ratchaprarop. Travel time from the airport to

Phayathai is about 30 minutes. The ticket fare begins at Baht 15 to 45 depending on the distance.

SA Express

The Express line has two service routes which are the yellow line and the red line. The yellow line has the ability take you from Suvarnabhumi Airport to the Bangkok City Air Terminal at Makkasan station within 15 minutes because it takes a straight trip bypassing all other stations. On the other hand, the red line takes about 18 minutes from the airport to Phayathai station, also bypassing the mentioned stations. However, because the Makkasan station is not connected to the BTS (Skytrain), you would stop and get off at the Phayathai station. Here you will find a link via walkway to Petchaburi MRT station or the city's underground/subway.

The SA Express only runs once every hour from 06.30 to 23.30. So, plan accordingly if rushing into the airport for a flight. The tickets for both lines are Baht 90 for a single trip and Baht 150 for a round trip.

Car Rental

At Suvarnabhumi Airport, you can find both well-known international and local car rental service providers located at Gate 8 on the 2nd floor of the Passenger Terminal. All services are available 24 hours a day.

- Avis Tel. 0-2251-1131-2

  www.AVISThailand.com

- Budget Tel. 0-2203-9251, 0-2203-0250

  www.budget.co.th

- Hertz Tel. 0-2266-4666

  www.hertzthailand.com

- Thai Car Rental Tel. 089-133-6126, 083-754-3399, 086-909-4422

Airport Tips and Warnings

Beware of unauthorized people trying to offer transportation or guide services. As at any airport in the world (save for a very few), it is not the wisest to deal with unauthorized people who may try to offer transport or guide services. The best place and people to get these sorted out is with your travel agent or contact agents registered with the Tourism Authority of Thailand or the Airports Authority of Thailand, or those displaying reliable international logos only.

No matter how harried or tired you are, try to pull from deep within you and make sure that you have all your luggage and or boxes loaded onto the hired car you decide to get before pulling out of the airport limousine/taxi queue. It is one hassle to have your luggage lost on-flight, quite another when it gets stolen, left behind on the asphalt or spirited away by some unknown person.

There have been many an instance when individuals have arrived at their destinations after a long flight, only to find discovers some of the luggage they had gathered from the carousel was not in the vehicle that had brought them to where they are. Should you need assistance relating to safety, unethical practices, or other matters, please contact the Tourist Assistance Centre on Tel. 0-2281-5051, 0-2282-8129.

Private Vehicles

Renting a car is common practice amongst expatriates (or their employers). These normally long-term agreements cover insurance, maintenance, car tax, etc.. These leased cars may also come with a driver making this option a more convenient choice than purchasing a car. To be able rent a car, the following documents need to be presented:

- Passport
- Credit card
- Driver's license

Drivers

Many expats still opt to employ drivers instead of driving themselves around. Good drivers are often found through word of mouth, references, recommendations, advertisements at expatriate locations (i.e. British Club, Villa supermarket on Soi 33 Sukhumvit), or through their employers. Unless you know someone who knows someone, it may take a while for you to locate a good, trustworthy driver.. An interim measure when you arrive is to hire a driver through a firm. We have listed a few places below for you to check out. Often these places would offer services of both car and driver.

Krungthai Car Rental

455/1 Rama III Rd., Bangklo,

Bangkholaem, Bangkok 10120

Tel. 0-2291-8888 ext. 130-133

www.krungthai.co.th

Unity Inter Marketing Co., Ltd.

4/506 Moo 4 Klongkum, Bungkum, Bangkok 10240

Tel. 0-2540-0640-43

www.unity-inter.com

Purchasing a Car

Now, if you are bent on owning and driving a car in Thailand, you will have to know and consider that cars are pretty costly acquisitions due to high taxes imposed on them. You would also be able to choose from second-hand cars which are also widely available. For detailed advice, visit this website www.siammotorworld.com.

For one to start the process of buying a car, here are the following documents which will need to be presented:

- o Copy of work permit (all pages)
- o Letter/proof of the expatriate's address in Thailand (obtained from embassy or local immigration office)

o Copy of passport (photograph page and current visa page)

- Roadside assistance service is available through the CarWorld Club Tel: 0-2612-9999.

- For general maintenance, you can contact either your car dealership or B-Quik service centre network Tel: 0-2789-3210 or www.b-quik.com.

- For repairs, a car dealership also provides these services.

- A garage would usually charge a fraction of the repair cost charged by car dealerships.

- You can contact Autobacs on Narathiwat Road. Tel: 0-2676-4370 for installation of in-car entertainment, tires, and accessories.

Driving License

To drive around Thailand you will have to be a valid Thai or and international driving license. A local Thai license can be obtained against your country's driving license. The following documents need to be submitted:

o Driving license from your home country or an international driving license (original and copy). A formal translation from the embassy is required for driving licenses that are not in English.

o It is recommended that you obtain an international driver's licence for driving licences that are not in English to avoid the process at the embassy.

o Passport with non-immigrant visa (original and copy). Individuals with tourist visas do not qualify.

o Work permit (original and copy) or present residential address in Thailand certified by your embassy.

o Medical certificate from a clinic or a hospital.

You will have to apply for a driving license in person. Take a Thai speaker with you, to help you translate and talk to officials, if possible. You will need to pass an eye test In order to get your Thai license. There is no driving test to pass. Contact the Department of Motor Vehicles Tel.1584

- The fee is 605 baht for cars and 355 baht for motorcycles.

- It usually takes a day to get the license, granted that you already have a driver's license in your country before.

- You will be provided with a non-permanent license which must be renewed after one year.

- After that, a permanent license is renewable every 5 year.

Car Insurance

Law stipulates that all vehicle owners be obliged to get compulsory government insurance. This insurance covers medical expenses and deaths brought about by accidents involving the insured vehicles, but this does not cover the vehicle itself. Motorists may want to acquire additional insurance coverage for vehicle repair costs brought about by accidents.

Driving in Thailand

o   Motorists drive on the left-hand side of the road.

o   A driver's license must be carried at all times.

o   The yearly vehicle tax certificate and a yearly compulsory insurance certificate must be displayed on the windscreen.

o   License plates are to be clean and attached to the car (front and rear).

o   The legal city speed limit is 80 km/h

o   Outside the city the speed limit is 90 km/h.

o The speed limit varies between 80 and 120 km/h on expressways and country roads.

o Drivers should pay special attention to speed signs posted on the left-hand side of the road for specified speed limits.

o Always buckle up. The law requires front seat passengers in cars to wear

o A seat belt; the maximum fine for not wearing a safety belt is Baht 500 each. In practice, however, the usual fine is Baht 200.

o Watch out for bumps, potholes, uneven roads and poorly-lit road construction sites.

o Watch out for motorcycles and cyclists, there are many of them in Bangkok.

o If riding a motorcycle, it is a legal requirement to wear a crash helmet.

o Don't be surprised and take case driving because in the event of an accident, the more affluent driver, even if not at fault, is frequently compelled to cover the expenses of the other party.

- o Motorcades of royal family members and VIPs are commonly seen.
- o Policemen may block the roads/expressways in order to give them right of way.

Expressways

The Bangkok expressway system runs directly above the main roads and motorists on these thoroughfares will go through a number of toll booths, but toll charges are normally only about 10 - 55 baht. Traversing the span of the expressway or between the city and a housing estate on the outskirts of the city, could rack up toll fee charges up to 70 baht or more per trip. Both cash payments and Easy Pass are accepted at these toll booths. The expressways of Bangkok may seem to be a quick alternative to your destination; however, there are times when congestion can be too much.

The Easy Pass is an electronic toll collection system which allow for easier payments at toll booths and is a system that is less time-consuming and outright convenient for the frequent traveller of the raised autobahns . Upon registering to the ease of use of the Easy Pass, the motorist will get a smart card which they can refill with mone; an Easy Pass device will then be installed on your windshield. This device will send and receive signals as you drive through toll booths. This saves you time having to fish for change, preparing money and stopping to pay toll fees. Conveniently, there are special lane(s) dedicated for Easy Pass.

In order to register for the convenient toll-payment service, provide a copy of your passport. Register and refill your Easy Pass at every toll plaza of the Expressway. You can get further information by contacting the Easy Pass call centre at Tel. 1543 or by visiting their website at www.thaieasypass.com.

Public Transport

No everyone can afford to purchase a car, rent one or even want to, and if you are this individual, fret not. There are a number of means to get around the cities of Thailand.

In Bangkok, public transportation is available and affordable. The availability of rapid public transportation helps the commuting individual to shorten their travel time commuting in the city> Because of the efficiency of the transport system in the city, this reduces the uncertainty of arriving on time at one's intended destination.

BTS

The BTS (Bangkok Transit System or the skytrain) started its operations in December 1999 and so many of the population of Bangkok, residents and tourists alike have felt the effects of the convenience of flitting from one place to the next in a time fashion. Check out the schedule for the trains regularly, there shouldn't be too many changes or delays. The BTS currently has a fleet of 51 four-car trains.

- During regular hours, trains generally run every five minutes.

- During rush hours, trains are scheduled to leave every 3-4 minutes.

- The system operates every day from 6am to midnight.

The BTS connects the most important business areas of Silom and Sukhumvit. The BTS network to other areas of Bangkok is under construction and is reported to have targeted to be in operation by 2018.

- Fares for the skytrain are priced between 15-52 baht for a one-way journey.
- Stored value cards can also be purchased at adult and student rates.

METRO (MRT)

The first subway line of the MRT in Thailand first came operational in July 2004. The first line covers 20-kilometres of the most heavily congested areas of Bangkok. These usually congested areas cover the span of the 18 stations though the completion of the envisaged network may not become apparent until 2020. The expansion plan in the works include an addition of 5 lines and more than 100 stations which covers most of Bangkok and some parts of the suburbs.

- Trains operate from 6 am to midnight.

- Fare cost ranges between 16-40 baht for adults

- Fare cost ranges between 8-20 baht for children and elders.

BRT

The BRT or the bus rapid transit system which has been operating since 2010 is another means of mass transport within the limits of Bangkok. The 16 km route has 12 stations between the terminals that link to two BTS stations of the Silom line:

- Chong Nonsi and the newly opened Talat Phlu. The bus runs along Narathiwat Ratchanakharin and Rama 3 roads.

- The bus fares ranges between 12-20 baht depending on the distance; every 2 stations cost approximately 2 baht more.

- BRT operates daily from 6am to midnight and comes every 5 minutes during peak hours and 10 minutes during off-peaks.

TAXI

Even with the availability of the BTS and subway, certain destinations are simply more easily accessible by taxi. On top of this, a taxi can fetch you from your location by arranging a home pick up service through the many call centres ready to take in your cab bookings. Call Tel: 1681, 1661, 0-2880-0888, 0-2676-1000, 0-2883-6621-5.

Note there is a 20 baht surcharge for taxis booked and rented via two-way radio. An advance notice of 20 minutes is advisable when using this service, but up to 30 minutes may be required during rush hours and also when the taxi shift changes between 3 to 4 pm.

Chapter Ten: Customs, Conducts and Thai Mannerisms

It goes without saying the Thai life and customs are a far cry from what many foreigners are not used to and may find strange or different. You are not alone. These are quite valid observations, even if the tables were turned. Customs and traditions can be a daunting, even unfamiliar, for anyone coming into a new country. Knowing how to interact with the locals early on into your move to Thailand is not only a smart thing to do, it is vital.

Being in the know opens you up to the opportunity to get into the step of your new host country.

Code of Conduct

In the West, and many other countries, we are used to be called by our surnames after the title Mr., Mrs., or Ms. this is quite different when in Thailand. The locals call each other by their first names, rather than using surnames. Historically, Thai's did not have surnames until about 100 years ago during the reign of King Rama VI. It was only during this time when citizens were encouraged to choose for their families a unique surname, resulting in the long surnames we are usually confounded reading, much less say. Therefore, the custom of calling each other by first name with the honorary word "Khun" which can mean Mr., Mrs., or Ms. at the beginning of the person's name has been the popular manner of how people address each other.

In most Asian homes, people remove their shoes when entering any house. So it goes when you enter a Thai house. Thai locals have customarily walked barefoot in their home for hundreds of years. However, most times there would be slippers provided for a guest. If invited for lunch or supper, you will notice that Thais do not eat with a knife or fork; instead they use a spoon and fork. In Thai culture, putting a fork into one's mouth is considered ill-mannered as this is akin to putting a knife in your mouth in Western cultures.

It is not uncommon, nor is it unusual for people of the same sex, to hold hands in Thailand, especially when they are close friends. It does not mean anything other than people enjoying the closeness of a platonic relationship. Thais have a way of greeting people called a "wai." This works much like what we are accustomed to in the West through shaking hands. Instead of shaking hands with a new person, Thais would place their press their palms together to their chest (like in prayer like movement) with a slight bow of the head.

Tradition, dictates that the younger person initiate the wait to a senior individual, and the senior would "wai" in acknowledgement. However it does not mean that the handshake has totally lost its meaning, since it is not unusual to witness handshakes in a business setting. To understand why some Thais give a limp handshake, know that many Thais are not used to the Western custom of shaking hands, much like westerners are unaccustomed to the "wai."

Thais traditionally have a hierarchy for the various parts of the body, with the head being the highest point and the feet at the lowest. Touching someone's head in Thailand is considered rude and disrespectful, unless, you are a monk. Monks are an exception as they are highly revered figures of society, much like the reverence and respect shown for the King or the Royal Family. These are the only acceptable people who can touch another person's head, as a way of giving blessing. Never point at something with your feet as this is considered disrespectful in Thai culture and because the feet are considered the lowliest part of the body.

You will note that Buddhist monks can be found almost everywhere in Thailand. Keep in mind that these figures are revered individuals of the Thai culture and they are prohibited from touching or being touched by a female, no matter the statues of the female. Should a monk be touched by a Buddhist female accidentally, this would be considered a grave infraction by the monk of their code of conduct. The monk would then have to owe up to the offense, no matter if it was accidental. On the other hand, the Buddhist woman would be considered to have committed a moral offense. A non-Buddhist woman is not castrated in the same way because they do not know any better, but the monk himself would still have to confess the offense and the rule will stand. So take great care, if you are a woman in Thailand, not to accidentally touch a monk.

Being part of the community of the area you choose to take up residence in Thailand will mean you will probably get invited to festive occasions. One such occasion would be a wedding. It would be important to remember to be practical when attending a Thai wedding, especially if you are invited to attend a morning ceremony Thai weddings and last for a notoriously extended of the day in conditions that are hot and humid. Be sure to wear comfortably smart, lightweight and Loose-fitting clothes. The morning ceremonies normally conclude around mid - day when refreshments are served and guests are given the opportunity for a change of clothes before the evening festivities and main reception begin. As a general rule, t-shirts, shorts or flip-flops are not allowed. It is also considered unlucky to wear black at a wedding therefore keep your black dress in the closet or your tux in the box. It is acceptable however for men to wear black shoes and black slacks.

Some weddings are more formal than others, most especially in the big cities like Bangkok. Those from affluent families and figures from high society will be dressed to the nines the invitation may require you to wear a suit and tie or an evening gown. On the other end of the spectrum attending a wedding at a rural Thai village would not require one to come in formal wear. Having on a suit or a gown at a village or beach wedding would be absolutely impractical not to mention uncomfortable.

Should you not be sure of what to wear do not hesitate to ask the person who extended the invitation about the dress code.

Superstitions

Every culture and society no matter they acknowledge it or not all forms of superstition and beliefs which they adhere to and follow. This too is true for Thailand. No matter how silly it may sound to you, your goal of integrating yourself, and your family into the Thai culture would hinge on the respect you extend to their beliefs.

It is considered unlucky to give any objects that are sharp to a Thai as a gift avoid giving scissors, knives, needles, or forks to a Thai. The Thais believe that this would cause severance of relationship between the recipient and the giver.

Giving handkerchiefs is also thought to be unlucky and will result in a tearful and sad separation of giver and receiver forever. Although the next superstition has somewhat faded, There are still a few who observed that Wednesday is not a good day for any sort of grooming. it is believed that whatever is clipped, cut, pruned and groomed on this day will not grow and will not prosper. This is the reason why sum barbers and salons choose to lock up on Wednesdays.

Stepping on a threshold most especially at a temple is believed to be about omen. It is held the guardian angel lives in the threshold and stepping on it will spark the ire of the angel and will bring bad luck to the person. You will notice that outside most Thai houses are little miniature houses. These are spirit houses. Most Thais subscribe to the belief that spirits are everywhere, Therefore If spirits are already in nature then spirits will also be present in homes. Hence the tiny house you see outside most Thai homes.

Useful phrases in Thai

Hello, Good-bye = Sawaddee

How are you? = Khun sabai dee mai

Thank you Kob khun

I'm sorry = Kor tord

Help! = Chuay duay

How much? = Thao rai

Expensive Paeng

Yes = Chai

No = Mai chai

Never mind = Mai pen rai

Good = Dee

Bad = Mai dee

I cannot speak = Thai Phuut Thai mai dai

I don't understand = Mai kaw jai

I understand = Kaw jai

Straight on = Trong pai

Turn left = Leaw sai

Turn right = Leaw kwa

Stop here = Yood, Jod

Slow down = Cha cha noi

Switch to the left hand lane = Chid sai

Change to the right hand lane = Chid kwa

U-turn = U-turn

PHOTO REFERENCES

Foreword Page Photo by user Patrik M. Loeff via Flickr.com,

https://www.flickr.com/photos/bupia/1466174731/

Page 1 Photo by user Tom Jutte via Flickr.com,

https://www.flickr.com/photos/hereistom/8098073040/

Page 4 Photo by user Rushen via Flickr.com,

https://www.flickr.com/photos/rushen/12214506556/

Page 11 Photo by user Tore Bustad via Flickr.com,

https://www.flickr.com/photos/torbus/24136780689/

Page 17 Photo by user Reinhard Link via Flickr.com,

https://www.flickr.com/photos/129472585@N03/16778611890
/

Page 27 Photo by user M M via Flickr.com,

https://www.flickr.com/photos/43423301@N07/3998448102/

Page 33 Photo by user Tom Jutte via Flickr.com,

https://www.flickr.com/photos/hereistom/8101130944/

Page 62 Photo by user Reinhard Link via Flickr.com,

https://www.flickr.com/photos/129472585@N03/16345629343/

Page 73 Photo by user Juan Antonio Segal via Flickr.com,

https://www.flickr.com/photos/jafsegal/15657931164/

Page 89 Photo by user Transformer18 via Flickr.com,

https://www.flickr.com/photos/71267357@N06/15618220171/

Page 116 Photo by user Tom Jutte via Flickr.com,

https://www.flickr.com/photos/hereistom/8103512973/

Page 139 Photo by user Ninara via Flickr.com,

https://www.flickr.com/photos/ninara/33528313641/

REFERENCES

25 Interesting Facts about Thailand – Samujana.com

https://www.samujana.com/25-interesting-facts-about-thailand/

An In-Depth Guide to Thailand Visas: Applications, Requirements, and Extensions - ThailandStarterKit.com

https://www.thailandstarterkit.com/legal/thailand-visa/

Brief History of Thailand – Adventure – Life.com

https://www.adventure-life.com/thailand/articles/brief-history-of-thailand

Guide to Thailand Etiquette, Customs, Culture, Business – Kwint Essential UK http://www.kwintessential.co.uk/resources/guides/guide-to-thailand-etiquette-customs-culture-business/

History of Thailand - NationsOnline.org

http://www.nationsonline.org/oneworld/History/Thailand-history.htm

How not to go Broke Living in Thailand – An Expat's Guide – PerceptiveTravel.com

https://perceptivetravel.com/blog/2017/03/03/living-in-thailand/

Living in Thailand – Expat Info Desk

https://www.expatinfodesk.com/expat-guide/deciding-on-the-right-country/top-expatriate-destinations/thailand/

Moving to Thailand – Expat Arrivals

http://www.expatarrivals.com/thailand/moving-to-thailand

Religion in Thailand – Facts and Details

http://factsanddetails.com/southeast-asia/Thailand/sub5_8b/entry-3212.html

Thailand – Wikipedia.org

https://en.wikipedia.org/wiki/Thailand

Thailand Immigration Guide - immiguides.com

http://immiguides.com/immigration-guides/thailand/

Thailand - The Land of Smiles – Thai.nu

http://www.thai.nu/information

Thailand Travel Tips – AdventureInYou.com

https://www.adventureinyou.com/travel-guides/thailand-travel-tips/

The Best 5 Places to Live in Thailand – International Living https://internationalliving.com/the-5-best-places-for-expats-to-live-in-thailand/

The people, culture and business practices of Thailand –
Expats in Bangkok

https://www.expatsinbangkok.com/article/the-people-culture-and-business-practices-of-thailand.html

Trouble in paradise: Thailand and the expatriate experience – Asian Correspondent

https://asiancorrespondent.com/2016/03/expats-thailand/

Types of Thai Visa - Thaiembassy.com

http://www.thaiembassy.com/thailand/thailand-visa-types.php